27,266

S0-AGL-794

THE KEY TO ART

THE KEY TO
BAROQUE ART

Juan-Ramón Triadó
Professor of Art History

Lerner Publications Company ♦ Minneapolis

The publisher wishes to thank Judith Akehurst, Professor,
Minneapolis College of Art and Design, for her assistance
in the preparation of this book.

This edition published 1990
by Lerner Publications Company
241 First Avenue North, Minneapolis, Minnesota 55401, USA

In association with David Bateman Ltd.
32-34 View Road, Glenfield, Auckland, New Zealand

LIBRARY OF CONGRESS CATALOGING-IN-PUBLICATION DATA

Triadó, Juan-Ramón.
    [Claves del arte barroco. English]
    The key to baroque art / Juan-Ramón Triadó.
    p. cm.—(The Key to art)
    Translation of: Las claves del arte barroco.
    "A David Bateman Book"—T.p. verso.
    "In association with David Bateman Ltd.... Glenfield,
Auckland, New Zealand"—T.p. verso.
    Includes index.
    Summary: Describes the history and main characteristics
of baroque art and examines numerous examples of the
painting, architecture, and sculpture of the period.
    ISBN 0-8225-2056-7
    ISBN 0-8225-2059-1 (pbk.)
    1. Art, Baroque—Juvenile literature. [1. Art, Baroque. 2. Art
appreciation.] I. Title. II. Series.
N6415.B3T7513 1990
709.03'2—dc20   89-34984
                                                      CIP
                                                      AC

A David Bateman Book

Printed in Spain
Bound in USA by Muscle Bound Bindery

1 2 3 4 5 6 7 8 9 10 99 98 97 96 95 94 93 92 91 90

INTRODUCTION

NICOLAS POUSSIN. *The Inspiration of the Epic Poet.* c. 1630-33. The Louvre, Paris.

"Ut Pictura Poesis"—"As is Painting, so is Poetry"—is one of the ideals of Baroque painters. The works of ancient writers, such as Ovid and Virgil, were favorites of Poussin. In this painting, Apollo is the god of poetry. He carries his lyre and is accompanied by Calliope, the muse of epic poetry. They are instructing a young poet who is being crowned with a laurel wreath, which is a symbol of literary success. The painting is a tribute from the artist to his friend, Giambattista Marino. Marino was a poet who, like most poets of the period, defended painting as one of the noble arts. The poet Lope de Vega wrote, "Marino is a great painter to listen to— Rubens, a great poet to look at."

Definition

The word "Baroque" appears to derive from the word "barocco," meaning a pearl of unusual and irregular shape, or from the term "baroco," a complicated logical deduction. Thus a mixture of irregularity and dark complexity make up what is known as "Baroque." The negative connotations of the word were already present in the definition given in the *Dictionary of the French Royal Academy* of 1740: "A baroque expression or figure—all that is irregular, extravagent, uneven," and persisted for quite a long time.

rancesco Milizia, in his *Dictionary of Fine Arts*, published in 1797, emphasized the negative sense of the word even more, by writing, "Baroque is the height of extravagance and an excess of ridiculousness."

By the middle of the 19th century, the anti-Baroque fever had abated, and there was a move toward considering Baroque as an important style. It was Heinrich Wölfflin who finally encouraged people to view Baroque style as a positive force. In 1888, he published a significant essay entitled "Renaissance and Baroque," in which, for almost the first time, Baroque was presented as a separate style with its own forms of expression, rather than as a degeneration from the greatness of the Renaissance.

Baroque is currently accepted as the style that dominated European art throughout the 17th century and for part of the 18th century. Some of its major characteristics are a desire to appeal to the emotions as well as to the intellect, an interest in dramatic spatial and lighting effects, and the use of different artistic media in combination. The unique character of Baroque style shows both the contradictions and the unity of the age in which it was born.

FRANCESCO BORROMINI. San Carlo alle Quattro Fontane, also called San Carlino. 1664-67. Rome. Borromini uses concave and convex forms to create an undulating wall. At the same time, the strong upward movement of the vertical accents seems to break the confines of the capping balustrade and continue into infinity. The effects of movement and unity with surrounding space make San Carlino one of the best examples of Baroque architecture.

Geography and Chronology

It is not difficult to follow the spread of Baroque style. The most influential center was Rome, where Baroque was largely an expression of Catholic thought. Closely linked to Rome by religious ties were the Hapsburg courts of Spain and Austria, Spanish cultural centers in

MAP OF THE WORLD OF BAROQUE ART.

Rome was one of the earliest centers of Baroque art and the one from which the style spread worldwide.

1. Mexico
2. Lima
3. London
4. Antwerp
5. Utrecht
6. Paris
7. Santiago de Compostela
8. Turin
9. Venice
10. Valladolid
11. Genoa
12. Lisbon
13. Madrid
14. Barcelona
15. Valencia
16. Rome
17. Naples
18. Seville

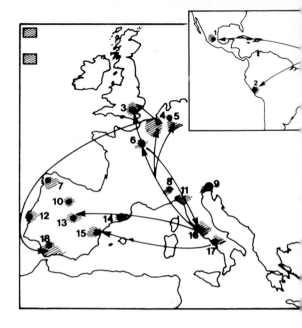

During the 17th century, Baroque style was dispersed throughout Europe by three distinct means: foreign artists coming to Italy and adopting Baroque as their new style; Italian artists traveling abroad and taking the style with them; and the works of art themselves, either originals or copies, which were sent to many places in Europe and in Central and South America. In Spain, Portugal, and France, art was closely linked to the ideology of the government. Dutch art Valencia, Toledo, Seville, and Madrid, as well a the Spanish protectorates of Naples, Lombardy and the southern Netherlands, or Flanders France stayed a little apart, avoiding the emotion alism of Italian Baroque, and creating an art more appropriate to the secular power of Louis XIV The Dutch Republic produced a rich heritage o largely middle-class, Protestant art, especially painting. Germany followed its own path toward the graceful, early 18th-century style known as **Rococo**. The Baroque styles in England, Portugal

was more often intended for private use and drew inspiration from Dutch traditions as well as from Italian models. In England, a combination of Dutch and Flemish influences flourished as English Baroque.

and the Spanish and Portuguese possessions in the Americas, however, were heavily influenced by foreign developments.

The chronology of Baroque art is complex, because its many variants make classification difficult. It is an especially difficult task to try to fix accurate dates for the beginning and end of the Baroque period. For example, a proto-Baroque style appeared in late 16th-century Italy, and **Mannerism** persisted well into the 1620s in Spain and northern Europe, especially in architecture. On the other hand, 17th-century artistic trends continued into the 1700s in Holland, but the new century saw a different approach to painting in England. Usage of terms complicates the issue still further. Some 18th-century works are called Late Baroque by some scholars and Rococo by

GIANLORENZO BERNINI. *Study for the Duke of Beaufort's Catafalque.* 1669. **The British Museum, London.**

Funerary monuments can express the taste of the period as well as commemorate the virtues and feats of the deceased. This memorial to the Duke of Beaufort, a French admiral, is enhanced with allegorical figures representing death and fame. The Christian hero stands on top of the pyramid, which is modeled on the Classical pyramid of Caius Cestus. Bernini has transformed the simple structure of the pyramid into a complicated and formal structure.

others. Also, social and political elements sometimes have as important a role to play as aesthetic ones in determining the length of the Baroque period in a given area. In 1700, the death of Charles II ended the Baroque period in Spain, and some scholars place the terminal date of French Baroque as 1715, the year of Louis XIV's death.

The Artist and Baroque Society

Baroque art can be defined as an expression of the ideals of established order. In 17th-century Europe, two distinct orders had been established—one that was that linked to the church and the royal courts and another that was linked to a more general public, often middle-

ss and Protestant. The first type accommo-
ted the needs and motives of the **patron**.
netimes whole teams of scholars and artists
rked together to produce a correct ensemble.
e extreme example of this approach to art is
rsailles, where the individual personalities of
ists were submerged into a grand program
rifying King Louis XIV. The second type of
roque art, destined for the open market, was
lded by fashion. Different types of subjects
pealed to buyers at different times, although,
general, middle-class audiences liked a realis-
style and subjects drawn from everyday life.
ese two poles, art dictated by ideas and art dic-
d by fashion, help to define the diversity found
Baroque art.

Both types presented certain problems for the
lividual artist. Since the Renaissance, philoso-
ers, painters, and others had argued that the

**GIANLORENZO
BERNINI. Sant'Andrea al
Quirinale. 1658-70.
Rome.**
The little church of
Sant'Andrea, built for Jesuit
novices, best sums up
Bernini's ideas about art.
It is a highly unified
composition in which
architecture, sculpture, and
painting combine to create
a religious setting of great
dramatic effect. The focus
of the interior is the high
altar, with its hidden light
source illuminating a painting by Guillaume Courtois
of the martyrdom of Saint
Andrew. Above, a sculpture
by Antonio Raggi shows
the saint being elevated to
glory by angels. Bernini is
said to have told his son
Domenico that he had a
special affinity for this
church and that he often
went there to find peace
of mind.

9

Program of paintings in the Hall of the Governors. 1634-35. Buen Retiro Palace, Madrid. (Reconstruction by J. Brown and J. H. Elliot in *A Palace for the King: Buen Retiro and the Court of Philip IV*.)
The paintings in the Hall of the Governors refer to the power of the house

visual arts were noble—on a plane with literatu rather than mere handicrafts. Yet the demands the patron on the artists who relied on comm sions and of the public on the artists who sc works on the open market influenced the artis freedom of expression.

The study of individual works helps the view to see the Baroque interest in creating highly ur fied works of art and in the interplay betwe various artistic media. Baroque architecture, f example, can become a **theatrum sacrum**, sacred theatre, a stage on which to display pair ing and sculpture. Especially in Italy, the integr tion of the arts can cause the viewer to feel like participant in a work, rather than solely a observer.

The theatrical nature of the Baroque is partic larly clear in works designed to commemora

event or person. Temporary architecture created to celebrate the visit of royalty or the more
permanent decorations of palaces and other
buildings show the Baroque emphasis on appropriate settings for important people and religious
ideas. In the kinds of works just mentioned, the
influence of the patron can be perceived. In some
cases, the patron was considered the real "artist,"
the one most responsible for a work's creation.
The Spanish writer on painting, Carducho, called
the Duke of Olivares the guiding genius behind
Buen Retiro.

of Hapsburg, which ruled
both Spain and Austria.
Military victories provided
subjects for many works
here; others have allegorical themes. The king of
Spain is shown as Hercules
in the center picture by
Francisco Zurbarán. Else-
where the king is identified
with the sun.

ARCHITECTURE

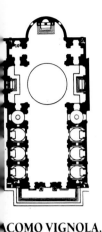

GIACOMO VIGNOLA.
Drawing from project for
church. 1568. Il Gesù,
Rome.

**GIOVANNI BATTISTA
GAULLI and
ANTONIO RAGGI.**
Ceiling Decoration.
1676-79. Il Gesù, Rome.

The project for Il Gesù
combined two artistic
concepts from different
periods. The first was con-
ceived in the plans of
Vignola and dates from the
beginning of the Counter-
Reformation in the 16th
century. Because of the
Counter-Reformation, the
reordering of the Catholic
Church that followed the
Protestant Reformation,
large spaces were required
in which to celebrate the
Eucharist and to read the
Gospels. From the end of
the 17th century, spiritual
experience was linked to
elaborate decoration. The

rchitects in the 17th century had two
goals—the creation of utilitarian spaces
and the creation of spaces that would
facilitate meditation. Baroque churches served
both purposes well. In the 16th century, the
reforms of the Catholic Church's **Council of
Trent** led to a need for large church buildings,
with fairly unified interiors, to accommodate
large congregations and to provide impressive
settings for the celebration of the sacraments as
well as for private prayer. The single-aisled basil-
ica, with its large central space, was the perfect
solution. Il Gesù is a good example of this kind of
church. It was designed by Giacomo Vignola for
the Jesuit Order, which became the vanguard of
the Counter-Reformation. The desire of the
Church to spread its message and advances in
technology encouraged later architects such as
Gianlorenzo Bernini, Francesco Borromini, and
Guarino Guarini to experiment with new forms,
which made interiors more conducive to meditation.

combination of sculpture
and illusionistic painting
transforms the ceiling into
a religious vision in itself,
suggesting the infinite.

13

FRANÇOIS MANSART and JACQUES LEMERCIER. Val-de-Grâce. Begun 1645. Paris.
GIACOMO DELLA PORTA. Drawing from facade of Il Gesù. 1571-75. Rome.
The facade of Il Gesù set a style which was soon followed by most Italian and French architects. It has three vertical sections. The two sides are lower than the center and are joined to the center by volutes, or scrolls. The center vertical section, containing the entrance, is the widest. Horizontally, the facade is divided into two sections topped by a large triangular pediment.

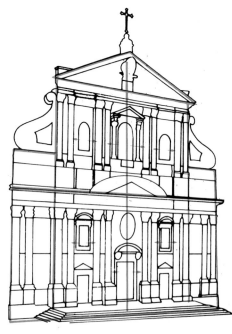

**GIANLORENZO BERNINI. Drawing from Santa Maria dell' Assunzione. 1662-64. Ariccia.
Drawing from Sant'Andrea al Quirinale. 1658-70. Rome.
BALDASSARE LONGHENA. Drawing from Santa Maria della Salute. 1631. Venice.
PIETRO DA CORTONA. Drawing from Santi Martina e Luca. 1635-50. Rome.
GUARINO GUARINI. Drawing from Santa Maria della Divina Providenza. c. 1698. Lisbon.**

Baroque churches come in many different shapes. Yet in them all—the circle of Santa Maria dell' Assunzione, the oval of Sant'Andrea, the octagonal of Santa Maria della Salute, the Greek cross (all arms of equal length) of Santi Martina e Luca, and the Latin cross of Santa Maria della Divina Providenza with its unusual oval bays or sections—the ideal of unified space is upheld.

At first, church facades continued to follow the Renaissance model of a two story structure with accented central section topped by a pediment. The bays, or individual sections of the facade, are defined by columns or pilasters, and a strong horizontal accent clearly separated the two stories. Early in the 17th century, however, certain important changes began to appear. The facade was no longer built in a single plane. The central section was closer to the street than the side sections, creating the impression that the facade was moving out into the urban space. Later, even greater alterations in the facade became common. Deep niches, free-standing columns, and other architectural elements gave the facade an almost sculptural appearance, while the extension of

15

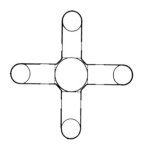

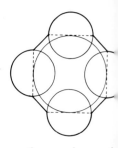

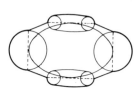

FRANCESCO BORROMINI. Drawing from San Carlo alle Quattro Fontane, also called San Carlino. 1634-91. Rome.
Borromini introduced geometric principles into Baroque architectural design. Here, two equilateral triangles, joined at their bases, seem to be the starting point of this plan, although some scholars have seen the underlying structure of the church as more complex and based on circles and ellipses.

decorative features, such as pilasters, beyond confines of a single story greatly increased sense of verticality.

Baroque architectural style aims toward t spatial integration. A theatrical sense of sp is created, with the separate elements dra together into a unified whole. The viewer cea to be merely an observer and becomes part of space itself. A good example of this experie can be found in San Carlo alle Quattro Font where Borromini introduced a plan with un lating walls composed of convex and conc lines. The viewer's eye is invited to follow alor

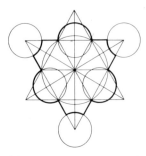

FRANCESCO BORROMINI. Drawing from Sant'Ivo della Sapienza. 1642-50. Rome.
The plan of the church of the ancient University of Rome is based on two superimposed equilateral triangles that form a six-pointed star, the symbol of wisdom. At the points of the star and the intersections of the triangles are circles which create a very dynamic spatial

design. Such Baroque structures depart from Renaissance practice, s they are based on geom in addition to numeric proportion.

FRANCESCO BORROMINI. Dome of Sant'Ivo della Sapienza. 1642-50. Rome.
This church provides a good example of the suggestion of continuous space. Borromini has succeeded in leading the eye from ground level up to the lantern of the dome, and beyond, for the dome appears to open out into infinity—an effect achieved by structural tricks. The spiral of the lantern also gives the building a kind of energy.

JULES HARDOUIN-MANSART. Complex of Les Invalides. c. 1679-91. Paris.

The overall scheme of the church (only the dome is visible in this photo) and other sections of Les Invalides exemplify the taste of the age of Louis XIV. The relative importance of Classical and Baroque influence on the French art of this period is a matter of controversy. However, the term Baroque is used to describe a design which has monumentality and a sense of upward movement. The double drum of the dome seen here does convey such a sense.

relentless, seemingly endless, surface, which ha no distracting features.

Baroque ideas on the use of space allowed for a number of different ground plans, all of them with highly unified interiors. Among the many option open to Baroque architects were circular, transverse elliptical, longitudinal elliptical, composite, elongated Greek cross, biaxial, and octagona plans. All were employed across Europe during the course of the 17th century.

Another consequence of the emphasis on spatial integration was the inclusion of the dome a part of the interior space rather than as a separate entity. The dome of Sant'Ivo della Sapienza in Rome, for example, has a spiral which draw the eye upward. The same relationship of part can be seen on the outside where the outline o the dome forms an integral part of the design.

Baroque buildings retained Classical elements of course. The decorative vocabulary, especially consisting of such features as columns and pediments, was taken from ancient architecture Borromini and later architects broke somewha with the Classical tradition by employing Late Antique, Gothic, and even Muslim forms in their works. Guarini justified the departure from Classical norms in his *Civil Architecture*. He pointed out that even some Roman buildings had not been constructed according to the rules that many 17th-century architects revered. He added, "Many new ideas of proportion and many techniques now exist which were unknown to the ancients."

Finally, certain regions developed their own individual characteristics in architecture. In Spain, for instance, the Flemish spire and unusual dome shapes gave churches a distinctive look.

Secular architecture was utilitarian but nevertheless retained some ideological content. Its buildings are functional and, at the same time, clearly demonstrate the status of their owners.

GUARINO GUARINI. Dome of the Church of San Lorenzo. 1668-87. Turin.
Here Guarini creates the impression of limitless space through crisscrossing arches in the dome. A star is formed at the center, through which dazzling light shines and enhances the spiritual dimension of the church.

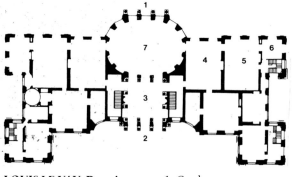

LOUIS LE VAU. Drawing from Vaux-le-Vicomte. 1657-61. Paris.
This château was built for Nicolas Fouquet, the French minister of finance for Louis XIV. The design itself is of an open nature, with a single axis leading from the entrance to the garden in back of the château.

1. Garden
2. Grand Entrance
3. Vestibule
4. Antechamber
5. Chamber
6. Cabinet
7. Salon

Secular architecture achieved its highest degree of development in Italy and France. The imposing city residence, called a *palazzo* in Italy and a *hôtel* in France, and its suburban or rural counterpart, the *villa*—in France the *château*—exemplifies this type of building.

These buildings may be studied individually or in context. Considered in isolation, the 17th-century Italian palazzo copies Renaissance models consisting of an enclosed space around a central court. There is a single entrance into the court, from which a staircase leads up to the most important floor, called the *piano nobile*. This main floor contained the *salone*, or great hall, or *salon* in French, the major public room of the palazzo.

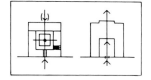

Sketch plan of an Italian Baroque palazzo and a French hôtel (after Norberg-Schultz).
The Italian palazzo, or important city residence, continued being built around a courtyard, as in the Renaissance. The courtyard of a French hôtel, by contrast, was

only an entrance. Like the country château, the hôtel had a sense of directed movement along a central axis.

GIANLORENZO BERNINI. First project for the east facade of the Louvre. 1664. Cabinet des Dessins, Paris. GUARINO GUARINI. Palazzo Carignano. 1679-92. Turin.

Bernini proposed an undulating wall for the facade of the Louvre in Paris. For the Palazzo Carignano, Guarini also employed curving elements, borrowed from Borromini's San Carlino. While the side sections of the palazzo, planned as blocks, negate the sense of openness which Borromini achieved with San Carlino, this facade influenced many 18th-century buildings in central Europe.

    This design evolved toward greater openness, however, with the construction of the Palazzo Barberini in Rome. Here the disappearance of the courtyard and the placement of a garden at the rear brings the plan closer to villa architecture or to the French hôtel. These new features also imply a greater involvement of the building with its surroundings, and, by extension, with civic life.

    The great change in palazzo facades can be seen in Bernini's first project for the Louvre in Paris. The sections of the facade are clearly defined but linked by an undulating movement of convex and

LOUIS LE VAU, CLAUDE PERRAULT, and CHARLES LEBRUN. East facade of the Louvre. 1667-70. Paris.
The east facade of the Louvre was based on ancient Greek and Roman buildings, drawn up in proposals from the Académie Française. Although the project was signed by François D'Orbay, the design was probably Perrault's; the facade is often referred to as "Perrault's Colonnade." The French taste for clearly defined forms and for an almost archaeological correctness in quoting from the architecture of ancient Rome—here a temple peristyle—can be found in the work of their architects throughout the century.

concave elements. Although the plan was never adopted, the concept of the undulating wall was taken up by Guarini in the Palazzo Carignano in Turin, a building which represents the culmination of developments in the Italian Baroque palazzo.

The progressive breakdown of Classical formulas by the introduction of elements such as undulating walls took place in Italy. It had little effect in France, where the emphasis in formality and clarity, achieved through the careful delineation of each part and of the relationship between

23

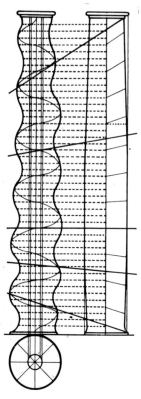

GIANLORENZO BERNINI.
The Baldacchino.
1634-33. Saint Peter's, Rome.

The Baldacchino is a paradigm of Baroque design. The use of monumental twisted columns give the impression of spiraling upward movement while the sheer size of the work expresses the power of the Church and the pope.

the part and the whole, prevailed. The east facade of the Louvre, based on models from ancient Greece and Rome, is considered by many the high point of French Classicism in architecture. The châteaux of Maisons by François Mansart, Vaux-le-Vicomte by Louis Le Vau, and, above all, the palace of Versailles also serve as excellent examples of French orthodoxy.

TOWN PLANNING

The desire of Baroque artists to incorporate disparate elements into a unified whole can also be seen in town planning. This period saw the development of the capital city, with Rome as the prototype. Improvements in Rome's layout had already begun in the early 16th century, but Pope Sixtus V and his chief

...n of Rome (after
...edion).

...tus V, who became pope
...1585, initiated a program
...own planning that
...ulated the growth of
...me through a coherent
...d system, the develop-
...nt of several public
...ares and monuments,
...d the improvement of
...water supply. His plans
...road construction facil-
...ed the growth of the city
...he north and east and
...ited the city's seven pil-
...mage churches, allowing
...faithful to visit them all
...one day.

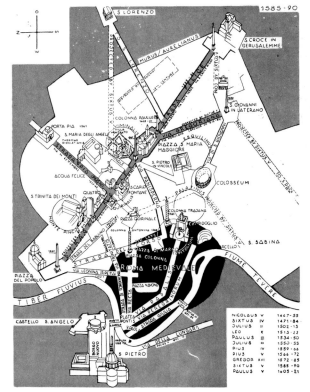

GIANLORENZO BERNINI. Saint Peter's Square. 1656-67. Rome.
Bernini, master of the Baroque style, combined three fundamental aspects of Baroque urban design here: the integration of space, the creation of framing elements, and symbolism. The semicircles of the colonnade blend into their surroundings, they serve as a frame for the facade of Saint Peter's, and they symbolize the welcoming arms of the Church.

architect, Domenico Fontana, were responsib for the most significant changes. Sixtus' city pl was based on a framework of main roads conne ing several buildings and *piazzas*, or square essential to the city's activity. Existing piazz were given new importance through the erectic of statues, fountains, or columns crowned wi

ures of Saint Peter or Saint Paul. These elements rved as focal points for the piazza, and the col-nns also initiated changes in the direction of ads. The orientation of Rome was now from e northwest, where the Piazza del Popolo arked the major entrance to the city, to the utheast, with the Strada Felice as the major axis.

JUAN GÓMEZ DE MORA. Plaza Mayor. 1620 (rebuilt 1672 and 1790). Madrid. JULES HARDOUIN-MANSART. Drawing from Place Vendôme. Begun 1698. Paris.
The Plaza Mayor was intended for all kinds of public gatherings. The Place Vendôme, on the other hand, was intended to glorify the king, Louis XIV, and to proclaim his generosity toward the arts by housing the various royal academies.

A piazza in Rome has a totally different signi cance from its French counterpart, the *pl* Piazzas in Rome form part of an overall pl whereas the Parisian place might be termed "isolated incident." The Piazza del Popolo, example, lies at the junction of three main stre leading into the city. Saint Peter's Square provi a place where the people may gather to rece the Pope's blessing.

In Paris, places developed individually ratl than as part of a general plan. Henry IV was t first French king to build places surrounded buildings with uniform facades, but even in l day, plans were by no means limited to the actu form of a square. Triangles, rectangles, and c cles were also used. As in Italy, monuments serv as focal points, but they usually related to the ki or to some aspect of royal administration rath than to the Catholic Church. The closest Itali parallel to a French square is the Piazza Navo in Rome, in part because of the uniformity of t facades of surrounding buildings.

An important aspect of Baroque town planni was the demolition of medieval walls and t

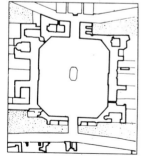

nsformation of the town into an open city. Paris minated its fortifications in the time of Louis V, replacing them with an almost complete ring boulevards. Christopher Wren's idealized plan London also sought to use the new openness connecting different parts of the city in a system of great crossing roads, with churches to be ilt at major intersections.

Baroque landscape design exhibits the same enness and integration of parts into a unified ole as that found in Baroque town planning. e greatest exponent of Baroque garden planng was André Le Nôtre. After developing his lls in the landscaping of Vaux-de-Vicomte, Le tre found great scope for his talents at Versailles d the Tuileries in Paris. He broke with the static angement of the Renaissance garden and ployed a great variety of elements, including mal beds, small groves of trees, fountains, ter courses, and ponds, all organized along a tral longitudinal axis. A garden planned by Nôtre combines order and openness and, in more extensive gardens, gives the impression infinite space. The grounds at Versailles, for ample, seem to stretch to the horizon.

LOUIS LE VAU, JULES HARDOUIN-MANSART, and ANDRÉ LE NÔTRE. Versailles. 1669-85.
Versailles should not be considered a juxtaposition of gardens and buildings, but a unified architectural composition, in which each part complements the rest. The palace is an integral part of the whole design, a part of the landscape itself.

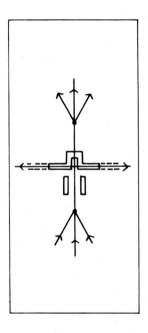

Conversely, nature, in Le Nôtre's gardens, seems to have been tamed and forced into a human design based on rational order. Thus, a rational space is created, which is in keeping with the structured and well-ordered society of 17th-century France.

STYLES IN THE PLASTIC ARTS

Throughout the 17th century, the **plastic arts** served three masters—the Catholic Church, the royalty, and the privileged class, whether noble or merely well-to-do. Each used art for its own benefit, which usually consisted of glorification or justification of status.

According to Weisbach, the image of the sacred in Baroque art is composed of five elements: mysticism (experiencing a communion with God), asceticism (self-denial as part of religious discipline), heroism, eroticism, and cruelty. These are the concepts directly related to the writings of great mystics—especially Saint Theresa of Avila (1515-77)—and works based on these ideas were intended to convert people by appealing to their emotions.

ANLORENZO RNINI. *Cathedra tri.* **1657-66. Saint ter's, Rome.**
e power of the Church s often expressed in inting and sculpture in e 17th century. In his *thedra Petri*, or Chair of ter, Bernini has com- ned Baroque style and eology. The bronze rone, encasing a 4th- ntury episcopal chair iditionally associated th Saint Peter, represents e authority of Christ ven to the popes. The rone seems to hang spended in midair. igels and religious mbols, such as the papal own and the keys to aven, complete the work hich stands above an :ar where the pope, ccessor to Saint Peter, ys the Mass.

GIANLORENZO BERNINI. *The Blessed Ludovica Albertoni.* **1674. San Francesco a Ripa, Rome.**
Bernini has managed to capture what he supposed to be the saint's state of mind at the moment of her death. Her ecstatic expression, showing a mystical union with Christ, is beautifully portrayed.

PETER PAUL RUBENS.
The Triumph of Truth.
**1622-25. The Louvre,
Paris.**

Baroque artists excelled in
making myths out of their
subjects. They glorify the
subject in form—by the use
of diagonals, full face portraits, and low viewpoints—
and in concept—by the use
of allegorical figures, such
as Time and Truth. Paint-
ings such as this portrait by
Rubens are really portraits
of power.

CLAUDIO COELLO. *The*
Adoration of the
Eucharist. **1690. Sacristy
of the Escorial
Monastery, Madrid.**

The connection between
the earthly power of the
king and the spiritual
power of the Church is
clearly seen in Coello's
series, *The Christian Prince.*
The work shown here links
the celebration of the
Eucharist with royal power,
and serves to confirm the
last Hapsburg king of Spain
as a champion of the Christian cause.

32

ALONSO CANO.
Immaculate Mary.
**c. 1655-56. Sacristy of
the Granada Cathedral,
Granada.**
The symbolism of the
Immaculate Conception
was a favorite theme of
17th-century painters and
sculptors, who represented
the Virgin Mary wearing a
white gown and blue cloak,
and surrounded by angels
with a crescent moon at her
feet.

A complementary viewpoint was expressed by
the Council of Trent, which recommended that
sacred art should be clear, concise, and easy to
understand, and that it should take full advan-
tage of its educational potential. It should be
realistically interpreted and should encourage
religious loyalty, appealing to the senses rather
than to the intellect. This aspect of Baroque art
found its truest expression in Naturalism.

The church used the plastic arts to assert its
new power as well as to instruct. There were many
representations of the pope, surrounded by personifications of the Virtues: Justice, Wisdom, For-
titude, Temperance, Faith, Hope, and Charity.

Other works, such as Bernini's *Cathedra Petri,* confirmed the pope's authority as God's representative.

Abstract ideas were represented in secular art, too. Images from mythology were often employed to represent the monarch's virtues, and the king was portrayed as Hercules or some other deity. Portraits and equestrian statues that make a display of royal power also exemplify this approach to art. Self-aggrandizement reached its peak in royal funerary monuments where earthly and spiritual values were joined "to the greater glory of the king."

The plastic arts of this period included works intended for the wealthy who were interested in

BARTOLOMÉ ESTÉBAN MURILLO. *Saint Francis and the Crucified Christ.* **c. 1668. Seville Provincial Museum, Seville.**
This is one of many examples of mysticism in Spanish art. Christ rewards Saint Francis's renunciation of all earthly things by releasing one arm from the cross to embrace him. Abstract ideas, like divine love and mystical union, are given concrete form.

MATTIA PRETI. *Martyrdom of Saint Sebastian.* **c. 1657. Capodimonte Museum, Naples.**
Heroism is combined with religious self-denial as Saint Sebastian's suffering is transformed by his love for Christ. The artist has employed many typical Baroque devices in the picture such as the diagonal formed by the saint's body and the low viewpoint which monumentalizes the subject and gives it a mythical quality. The powerful modeling of the figure itself, together with a certain morbid quality in the representation, tend to distance the viewer from the saint who has become an ideal Christian.

NICOLAS POUSSIN.
The Triumph of Flora.
**1631. Staatliche
Gemäldegalerie,
Dresden.**
Poussin was known for taking his subject matter from Ovid's *Metamorphoses*. Classical literature was often debated and interpreted by artists and intellectuals of the period. The space is rationally organized with the goddess Flora at the center scattering blossoms. Each of the other figures represents a character in Ovid's text who was changed into a flower because of some obsession or inordinate passion. The whole scene is an abstract study of human psychology.

self-assertion and for **dilettanti** who used thes arts to explore their own intellectual interests.

The Dutch Republic was a major commercia center whose wealthy middle class wanted to se their own world in works of art. The categorie of painting, such as landscape, still life, and grou portraits flourished in this society. Genre paint ings, or scenes of everyday life, displayed the pos sessions and daily activities of the Dutch middl class while landscapes and cityscapes faithfull reproduced the appearance of their countrysid and towns.

To a certain extent, stylistic trends in Baroqu art can be associated with these groups anc movements: Naturalism expressed the ideas o the Counter-Reformation, mainstream or Higl Baroque glorified the power of kings and popes Realism pleased the middle class, and an abstrac form of Classicism appealed to the intellectuals

SCULPTURE

GIANLORENZO BERNINI. *Tomb of Urban VIII.* **1628-47. Saint Peter's, Rome.**
Urban VIII gave Bernini his grandest commissions, and thus it is not surprising that the artist lavished so much care on this pope's funeral monument. The pope's authority is symbolized by his position atop the tomb, dispensing benediction to the faithful. Below, the figure of Death immortalizes Urban VIII by writing his name in gold letters on a scroll. On either side stand personifications of virtues—to the left is Charity or Love, the greatest of the Virtues according to Saint Paul, and to the right is Justice. The contrast in color between the materials used for the various figures gives this sculptural monument something of the effect of a painting.

Like Baroque architecture, Baroque sculpture began in Italy. The greatest sculptor was the versatile Bernini, whose work exemplifies that perfect blend of form and content, of style and idea, sought by artists of the period. Bernini's studio in Rome became a center from which his ideas and practices spread across Europe.

37

**IANLORENZO
ERNINI.** *David.*
**623-24. Borghese
allery, Rome.**
he capturing of a dramatic
toment, the creation of a
ense of evolution or becoming, and the estab-
lishment of a clear relation-
ship between spectator and
sculpture are three fundamental aspects of Bernini's
David. Here the viewer
seems to stand between David and an imagined
Goliath, becoming a partic-
ipant in the action. The
viewer's physical and intellectual involvement is
common in Baroque art.

Other schools of sculpture existed, but these
vere connected with the special needs of partic-
lar regions. In France, an extremely formal Aca-
lemic Classicism was used to celebrate the abso-
ute monarchy, while in Spain, Naturalist images
vere produced for the Church.

The materials used by sculptors varied accord-
ng to the place in which the work was produced.
n Italy, marble, alabaster, and bronze were pri-
narily used for works that would be placed inside
churches. With these materials, sculptors could
lisplay their great technical abilities, especially
since the blocks of stone were comparatively soft
and fragile. Bernini achieved a high degree of skill
n working in stone with his early works. Later,
he used highly innovative combinations of mate-
ials, as in the *Tomb of Urban VIII*, where the composition was complemented by the color scheme.
Bronze was used for the figures of the Pope and
Death, gilded bronze and black marble for the
stone coffin, and white marble for the figures of
Charity and Justice.

Stone was the preferred material throughout
Europe for works to be placed in the open air.
Fountains, like those by Bernini in Rome, are
made of stone, as are the facades of buildings,
statues in external niches of buildings, public
monuments, and sculptures adorning bridges.

In Spain, and in areas influenced by Spain, the
16th-century tradition of wood sculpture continued into the 17th century; statues were made

**JUAN PERUTXENA.
Santa Eulalia. 1644.
Barcelona Cathedral
Treasury, Barcelona.**
The dominant role of the
church in 17th-century
society made it one of
the main patrons of art.
Churches were filled with
images of the Virgin Mary
and of saints, particularly
local saints. This silver
gilt statue of Eulalia,
patron saint of the city
of Barcelona, shows the
wealth of the city as well as
the use of precious materials in sculpture.

39

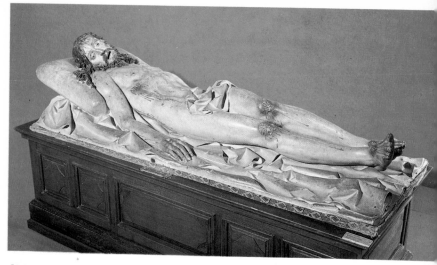

GREGORIO FERNÁNDEZ. *Christ Recumbent*. **Early 17th century. Museum of Sculpture, Valladolid.** Fernández, clearly showing the cruelty of the executioners, demonstrates a realistic approach designed to inspire deep religious feeling. The work involves the spectator emotionally.

GIANLORENZO BERNINI. *The Ecstasy of Saint Theresa*. **1645-52. Santa Maria della Vittoria, Rome.** Architecture, sculpture, and painting are brought together here into a dramatic unity. Saint Theresa is overcome by divine love in the symbolic form of a golden arrow held by an angel.

almost exclusively of wood. Wood sculpture, usually colored, filled the backs of altars and lined procession ways, becoming a specifically Spanish art form. Statues dressed in fine robes were also common throughout the Spanish-speaking world and at the court of Naples, which was a dependency of Madrid during this period.

Ivory, gold, and silver, were also used by Baroque sculptors. Stucco appeared in decorative works. Paper and cardboard were used for temporary, lightweight works, such as the images carried in parades during **Holy Week**.

There are two distinct forms of sculpture: relief sculpture, in which figures emerge from a flat surface, and sculpture in the round, in which fully three-dimensional and free-standing figures are created. Both forms can be found in Baroque art. Reliefs were often narrative in content. Individual figures were usually carved in the round. Sometimes relief and free-standing sculpture were combined in a single monument meant to be seen from just one side. This selection of one optimum viewpoint links Baroque sculpture with

that of the Renaissance and represents a depa ture from Mannerist practice, which allowed f multiple viewpoints.

Bernini and his followers rejected Michela gelo's definition of sculpture as "that which done by means of subtracting." The dynamic, int grated effects sought by Baroque sculptors cou not be achieved by carving a single large bloc Bernini also shunned the static ideal of beau espoused by the Renaissance in favor of mo active figures. He wished to capture a sing moment in time and to involve the viewer his works.

The emphasis on action and on a single view point indicate a major feature of Baroque art theatricality. Most works of the period lose the original meaning if separated from their intend environment. It is difficult to imagine Bernin *Saint Theresa* away from the Cornaro Chapel Rome, for instance. Similarly, images intended f religious or royal processions lose their comm nicative power in the cold gallery of a museum. Baroque work was made to be contemplated in specific setting, and on a personal level with t viewer. Baroque architecture served sculpture stage scenery serves a play.

Bernini was the most gifted creator of the theatrum sacrum with a skillful mix of architecture, painting, and sculpture, including the use of light and shade as symbolic elements. The sense of drama is particularly marked in the Cornaro Chapel where members of the family seem to watch the unfolding story of Saint Theresa from either side of a "stage." This suggestion

a theatrical setting reinforces the artist's message.

Baroque sculpture has four main kinds of subject matter—religious, mythological, allegorical, and civil, or relating to the state and its people—though different themes were sometimes combined in the same monument. Religious works often drew on the Bible or on church doctrine for their imagery. Because of Protestant concerns about **idolatry**, religious sculpture was concentrated in Catholic countries. Sculpture dealing

symbolic and a teaching role. Several different formats were used, but the most common arrangement consisted of horizontal sections combining statues with painted carvings in relief.

G. B. THÉODON. *The Triumph of Religion over Heresy*. Il Gesù, Rome. Théodon's grouping shows the immense power of the Church. Religion, a standing female figure, defeats Luther and Calvin, who were Protestant theologians, while an angel tears up what was considered to be a heretical book. The group stands near the altar dedicated to Saint Ignatius Loyola, and is balanced by another sculpture, *The Triumph of Faith over Idolatry*, also the work of a French artist, Pierre Legros. The two works refer to the defense of Catholicism and the spreading of the faith by the Jesuits, champions of the Counter-Reformation.

FRANÇOIS GIRARDON.
Apollo Tended by
Nymphs. 1666.
Versailles.

Group sculptures origi-
nated in ancient Greece.
Girardon's work was
inspired by Roman models
and copies of certain Greek
statues he had seen while
visiting Rome. The clarity
of the arrangement is
reminiscent of Poussin's
rational approach to com-
position. This work formed
part of the overall thematic
program of Versailles
which identified Louis XIV
with Apollo, the sun god.
Louis was actually called
the "Sun King."

with mythological themes appeared most oft
in France and usually referred to the king. All
gorical figures could be found in a variety
contexts, and were most popular on funera
monuments where the imagery of religious bel
and secular power were combined. Portrai
often used for Baroque civil sculpture, sometim
had religious and mythological undertones. T
best examples of civil sculpture can be found
France during the reign of Louis XIV and in Rom

Thus, sculpture was a vehicle for the expre
sion of ideas in the Baroque period, and ofte
formed part of a larger artistic program. Becau
sculpture was so closely related in theme an
composition to the other arts, especially arch
tecture, it is difficult to study the medium in is
lation. The same is true of painting.

PAINTING

Baroque painting is one of the richest and most varied products of the 17th century. Large paintings on canvas as well as frescoes, which are paintings done on wet plaster, adorned the walls, ceilings, and domes of churches and palaces throughout Europe. As a result of the Baroque interest in unified spaces, these works were planned for particular contexts. The removal

ANNIBALE CARRACCI. *The Loves of the Gods.* 1597-1604. **Palazzo Farnese, Rome.**

This ceiling painting, based on Ovid's *Metamorphoses*, refers to the power of love which overcame even the gods of antiquity. The mythological theme of the work and the great vitality of treatment indicate a relaxation of the strict morality of the Counter-Reformation.

of portable pieces from their original surroundings diminishes our understanding of them and their function.

45

MICHELANGELO MERISI, IL CARAVAGGIO. *Death of the Virgin.* 1605-06. The Louvre, Paris.

Caravaggio's extreme Naturalism is displayed in this moving representation of the dead Virgin Mary. Light bathes the figure of Mary as the Apostles openly grieve. Caravaggio is said to have used the corpse of a drowning victim as a model for Mary. The Apostles are also portrayed quite realistically as rustic men with dishevelled hair and bare feet.

PIETRO DA CORTONA. *Glorification of the Reign of Urban VIII.* 1633-39. Palazzo Barberini, Rome.

In this work, Cortona made use of **quadratura**, or the illusionistic enhancement of architecture. The ceiling is painted with the viewer's position in the room below taken into account, so that the elaborate framework and figures are convincingly represented. The decorative program was designed by the poet Francesco Bracciolini and brings together allegorical and mythological figures in a dramatic scene glorifying the Barberini pope, Urban VIII.

That same diversity of theme found in B[a]roque sculpture exists in 17th-century paintin[g]. Religious works, often quite large in scale, we[re] placed behind the main altar of a church or ov[er] the altars and on the side walls of chapels. The[se] paintings were intended to persuade worshippe[rs] of the validity of the Church's doctrines and provide subjects for prayerful meditation.

In secular settings, mythological and allego[ri]cal painting served different purposes. The pain[t]ings might appeal to the intellect of the viewer, [as] did Annibale Carracci's ceiling in the Palaz[zo] Farnese in Rome, or they might glorify a rul[er]

NICOLAS POUSSIN.
Rebecca and Eliezer at the Well. **1648. The Louvre, Paris.**
Well-defined groups, an emphasis on gesture, and underlying geometry are typical aspects of Poussin's style. In this setting of a passage in Genesis 24 where Abraham's servant meets his master's future daughter-in-law, Rebecca, the artist dwells on the psychology of the moment and the response of the human heart to God's grace. This scene could almost be interpreted as a foreshadowing of the **Annunciation** in the New Testament.

as did the decorations of the public rooms Versailles. Portraits, too, were an important pa of what can be called "palace art." Painters tende to make the subject of a portrait look grander more powerful.

The well-to-do, who were not necessarily nobi ity, also liked to decorate their homes and inst tutions with pictures. Large group portraits hur in town halls and the public rooms of building owned by guilds and other societies. The small rooms of private houses called for smaller work

Holland, especially, these pictures were often
familiar scenes from everyday life.

Baroque painting in the 17th century can be
divided into five stylistic categories, each domi-
nating a particular period or region: Classicism,
Naturalism, Realism, Academic Classicism, and
High Baroque.

Classicism, of which Carracci was the initia-
tor and principal exponent, represents that
current which ran counter to the excesses of
Mannerism and marks the transition from

GEORGES DE LA TOUR.
Saint Sebastian Attended
by Saint Irene. **c. 1650.**
The Louvre, Paris.
Georges de La Tour should
not be thought of strictly as
a Realist. The figures of his
mature style are somewhat
abstract when compared to
those of an artist like
Caravaggio. The closed
nature of this painting, the
lack of descriptive detail,
and the generalized fea-
tures of the figures attest to
the artist's interest in
formal values. Light helps
to link the figures in this
extremely introverted portrayal of a religious subject.

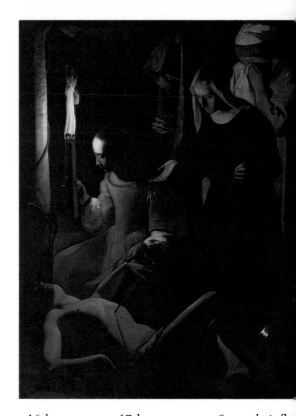

16th-century to 17th-century art. Strongly influenced by Renaissance and Venetian models, Classical painters stressed technical mastery and a
idealized treatment of major religious and mythological themes. The latter characteristic made
Carracci a strong opponent of Caravaggio's Naturalism, but both artists wanted to break away
from the Mannerist style, which had become
decadent.

Later in the century, a more intellectual variety
of Classicism was practiced by Nicolas Poussin.
The emotional distance and the emphasis on
order and drawing technique found in his work
seem at odds with the typical Baroque freedom
of composition and emotion. Bernini summed up
Poussin's approach when, tapping his forehead,

said, "There is a man who uses his head." Because of Poussin's concern with technical mastery, debate began in the French Academy of Painting and Sculpture over the relative merits of line and color in painting. Champions of line were called "Poussinistes," while the advocates of color were dubbed "Rubenistes," after the Flemish painter, Peter Paul Rubens.

Naturalism, like Classicism, was a reaction against Mannerism, but it was manifested in a different way. Naturalist painters used everyday people as models and brought religious and historical scenes closer to real life. Even so, their works were often open to symbolic interpretation. The lack of idealization constituted an artistic revolution at the time.

DIEGO VELÁZQUEZ.
Old Woman Cooking Eggs. **1618. The National Gallery of Scotland, Edinburgh.**
This sort of picture, which could be interpreted symbolically or as straightforward still life, was not much prized in 17th-century Spain. But the commercial character of Seville meant that two native painters, Velázquez and Murillo, produced works of great quality in this vein.

51

JUAN DE VALDES LEAL.
In Ictu Oculi and *Finis Gloriae Mundi.* 1673.
Hospital of Charity, Seville.

Three of the best artists in Seville—Murillo, Pedro Roldán, and Valdes Leal—were commissioned to decorate this hospital. Valdes Leal was entrusted with the inevitability of death and the Last Judgment. In the painting on the left, Death is seen extinguishing Life, represented by a candle. All earthly possessions, such as the crowns of the king and the pope, are revealed as worthless. In the painting on the right, the ultimate fate of all worldly power is represented by the rotting corpses of a churchman and a prince.

The most important Naturalist painter wa Michelangelo Merisi, Il Caravaggio, but there i great disagreement over the nature and extent c his influence. Some scholars claim that his exam ple shaped all subsequent Naturalist/Realis painting, while others deny that his influence wa that widespread. It must be admitted that th **chiaroscuro**, or the strong contrast of light an shade, for which Caravaggio is known, can als be found in some Venetian and Late Manneris works. Perhaps it would be safest to say tha he made realism and dramatic lighting effect popular.

In any case, Caravaggio did have followers The Dutch School of Utrecht, a few Spanish paint ers, and a wide circle of Italians all imitated hi style. Works by so-called "painters of reality" i France, however, often did not resemble Caravag gio's works. Georges de La Tour's mature styl for example, could be described as speculative o theoretical rather than realistic.

Realism was most popular in the Dutch Re public. Realist painters, like the Naturalists, drew their subjects from everyday life, but the Realist

FRANCISCO ZURBARÁN. Drawing from *Still Life with Oranges.* 1633. The Norton Simon Foundation, Pasadena.
JUAN SÁNCHEZ COTÁN. Drawing from *Still Life.* 1603-04. Granada Museum, Granada.
JAN FYT. Drawing from *Still Life with a Dog and a Cat.* Prado Museum, Madrid.
JUAN VAN DER HAMEN. Drawing from *Still Life.* 1623. Prado Museum, Madrid.

ended to give much more attention to detail. They created works which faithfully reproduced typical scenes of contemporary life–landscape, festivals, domestic interiors, etc. Some critics maintain that such Realist art reflects a self-absorbed society more concerned with personal success and wealth than with religious values. These scholars see the multiplicity of details in a Realist painting as the aesthetic equivalent of a stress on individual interests in society. However, interpreting these paintings is more complex than one might suppose, for many Dutch pictures have a secondary meaning which refers to moral or religious concepts.

Academic Classicism developed in Louis XIV's France and was tied to the fortunes of the Royal Academy of Painting and Sculpture. Because of the uniformity imposed on artists in both subject matter and treatment, this trend can seem repetitive and boring. However, it did lead to the creation of a national style, called–not surprisingly–the Louis XIV style. The example of an academy for the training of artists was widely copied throughout Europe in the 18th century.

These examples illustrate different approaches to still life. Zurbarán invested each element with a deep meaning, here referring to the Virgin Mary. The cup of water represents purity, the oranges and the blossom stand for virginity and fertility, and the rose symbolizes divine love. Sánchez Cotán experimented with form. The geometric treatment of the objects and their somewhat exaggerated arrangement should be viewed analytically. Jan Fyt was more concerned with the overall effect of his work than with the details. Van der Hamen gave each object its own individual character.

PIETER DE HOOCH.
The Linen Cupboard.
1663. Rijksmuseum, Amsterdam.
A contemporary of Vermeer, de Hooch painted many scenes of Dutch middle-class life. His spotless interiors and neatly dressed figures show the value the Dutch middle class placed on order and cleanliness.

The fifth stylistic category is **High Baroque**, which Rubens was a leading practitioner. H works embody many of the characteristics th are thought of as typically Baroque, including concern with the entire composition rather tha with the individual details, as well as a dramat quality quite different from the analytical spir prevailing in the Classical movement. Rubens interest in unity can be related to developmen in Baroque architecture, town planning, an sculpture.

REMBRANDT VAN RIJN.
The Carcass of Beef.
1655. The Louvre, Paris.
This astonishing work is
one of the most unsenti-
mentalized studies of real-
ty ever painted. Today its
artistic value can be
appraised as pure form,
and can be appreciated for
the powerful handling of
the carcass and the light
which accentuates it. In the
17th century, it probably
would have been appreci-
ated more for its references
to the crucifixion of Christ.
The thick brushwork used
here, with the paint applied
in blobs to obtain the effect
of relief, foreshadows European Expressionism.

The diversity of painting styles was accompanied by a great variety in the ways certain themes
were treated and by the preference for one kind
of theme over another during a particular period
or in a particular region. Religious works for
courts, churches, and monasteries naturally
predominated in Catholic countries. Still-life
painting, genre scenes, and flower pieces, on the
other hand, were most popular in the northern
Protestant countries.

Still-life painting takes various forms: realistic,
decorative, symbolic, and speculative. Realistic
still life emphasizes the individual appearance of
the objects depicted and presents them in a

JAN VERMEER. *View of Delft.* 1658-60. **Mauritshuis Museum, The Hague.**

Vermeer has captured the atmosphere and orderliness of Dutch society. The main subject of the painting is the town itself and how it looks in the sunshine after a storm.

Vermeer's attention to light has given the picture qualities that have sometimes been compared to those of 19th-century Impressionist painters. The little town of Delft has more than formal interest here, though; it also displays the benefits of Dutch middle-class society.

detailed manner. The decorative High Baroque still life, on the other hand, stresses the whole the overall effect, instead of the separate parts. The greatest representatives of this kind of still life were the Flemish and Neapolitan painters. Symbolic still life goes beyond the depiction of objects for their own sake to give these elements a deeper meaning. Francisco Zurbarán's *Still Life with Oranges*, for instance, was intended as an homage to the Virgin Mary. Speculative still life treats objects as abstract forms. The elements do not take on symbolic meaning but have been used as a basis for study.

Genre painting, or scenes of everyday life, also took a variety of forms. Some had a disguised religious or ethical meaning. Others contained no symbolism as such, but did appeal to the social attitudes and prejudices of the intended viewer.

he **bambocciate**, small paintings produced by
mostly northern European artists working in
Rome, for example, portray the lower classes as
picturesque, often violent, and/or ridiculous.

Domestic scenes involving the Dutch middle
classes show a much more serene and orderly
world. Both types of genre catered to the beliefs
of their audience.

Flower paintings have become the subject of
controversy. Some scholars see them as wholly
symbolic, referring to religious figures or provid-
ing moral messages about the passage of time and
the transitory nature of life. Yet these paintings
are undeniably decorative as well. Spanish flower
pieces became things of great luxury and ele-
gance, contrasting strongly with the austerity of
Spanish life in general. The most prestigious
17th-century school of flower pieces was in
Flanders, the southern portion of the Netherlands, or modern Belgium.

Landscape is yet another type of painting that
flourished in the Baroque period. Landscapes

MEYNDERT HOBBEMA.
*The Avenue, Middel-
harnis.* **1689. National
Gallery, London.**
Landscapes are one of the
great achievements in
17th-century art, and the
Dutch were particularly
gifted in this kind of painting. This simple composi-
tion is seen from almost
ground level, an appropriate way of depicting the flat
Dutch countryside. One
quarter of the painting is
devoted to the land, three
quarters to the sky and
clouds.

with Classical themes enjoyed their greatest pop-
ularity in France. Claude Lorrain is the best
known of the Classical landscape painters. He
attempted to capture on canvas the atmosphere
and light of a given moment as well as to create a
kind of nostalgia for the ancient world. The Dutch
preferred a more realistic approach. In Holland,
seascapes, which often referred to trade, and cityscapes or townscapes were important variations
on landscape. Some of Jan Vermeer's finest work
can be found in his views of Delft, which, like
interior scenes, show the pride of the Dutch in
their surroundings and possessions.

Portraits, too, were widely produced in the 17th
century. These express something of the confi-
dence and beliefs of the person or group being

ANTHONY VAN DYCK.
Charles I, Hunting.
c. 1635. The Louvre, Paris.
This portrait is set in an open landscape with the figure of the king silhouetted against the sky, while those of his groom and horse have become part of the background. The artist has portrayed the English king as a country gentleman rather than as an imperious ruler. It was probably just such a relaxed approach that earned this Flemish artist, who had worked in Rubens's studio, an English knighthood. Certainly his approach captured the hearts and imaginations of the great 18th-century English portraitists, who followed Van Dyck's example.

ainted. Portraits of people who were self-made ommunicate a certain pride of accomplishment. oyal and court portraits, on the other hand, were esigned to glorify the subjects. Sometimes Baoque artists used dynamic compositional techiques to convey the impression of greatness. In is *Pope Innocent X*, however, Diego Velázquez chieved the same result by relying mainly on killful characterization. Anthony Van Dyck's ortraits of Charles I of England also reveal the nan without losing sight of the king.

Family portraits were painted by nearly all the reat artists of the 17th century. In *Las Meninas*, elázquez produced one of the most modern orks by introducing ambiguity into the standard format. In the painting, he included images

REMBRANDT VAN RIJN.
The Night Watch.
**1642. Rijksmuseum,
Amsterdam.**
The novelty of the composition lies in its sense of life and movement. The interplay of color and light are extraordinary. The red sash and yellow uniform of the two major figures at the center of the composition provide the main tones, which extend outward into a series of scarlets, oranges, and tans.

of the young princess and her entourage, of himself at work, and of the king and queen reflected in a mirror, thus obliging the spectators to ponder the relationship between pictorial and physical reality and to redefine for themselves the meaning of the term "portrait."

Portraits of groups other than families were most popular in Holland. Societies, guilds, and the like all wished to be immortalized on canvas. Pictures of these self-confident men and women have come down through history in works by Frans Hals, Rembrandt van Rijn, and a host of minor artists. Unlike kings, the subjects of these group portraits do not pretend to be heroes, only successful people proud of their positions.

PETER PAUL RUBENS.
Hélène Fourment and Her Children. 1636-37. **The Louvre, Paris.**
Hélène Fourment, Rubens's second wife, embodied an ideal beauty in the eyes of the artist; her robust form became the model for female figures in most of his later works. In this picture, Rubens has captured a particular moment in time and a sense of family intimacy. Only the young boy seems aware of being watched and turns toward the viewer. The free brushwork, almost sketchy in the treatment of details such as the chair, is typical of Rubens's style.

Some painters used the self-portrait to proclaim their own importance and success. In *Las Meninas*, for example, Velázquez painted himself wearing the insignia of the Order of Santiago. This kind of self-assertion was intended to impress the artist's peers, but it also testified to the important role played by the artist in society. Other painters presented themselves in a more personal, intimate way, in the circle of their families.

Mythology, history, and allegory conclude the list of popular Baroque themes. All could be made to serve the established order. The gods of Classical mythology sometimes formed part of philosophical works, but they more often became instruments for extolling the attributes of the

DIEGO VELÁZQUEZ.
The Surrender of Breda.
1634-35. Prado Museum, Madrid.
Historical paintings can be pompous, but Velázquez introduced a refreshing realism into this portrayal of an actual event. He avoided any mythological characterization and concentrated on the human dimension. The victorious general seems most concerned with preventing the humiliation of the defeated general.

PETER PAUL RUBENS.
Drawing from *The Rape of the Daughters of Leucippus*. c. 1618. Alte Pinakotek, Munich.
The interplay of opposing curves and the use of diagonals are fundamental to Baroque style. Rubens arranges this dynamic whole within a geometric shape—the circle.

king. History, too, was presented as a record the great and virtuous deeds of the hero, wheth saint, pope, or king. Allegorical figures usual appeared in religious contexts, such as funera monuments, where they proclaimed the grea ness of both secular rulers and princes of th church.

Decorative programs, or series of works, royal palaces combined mythology, history, an allegory as to portray the monarchy as part of a unchanging and eternal order. The palace of Bue Retiro, for example, is a hymn to the glory of th Spanish royal house. The founder of the dynas was represented as Hercules and glorified in series of paintings by Zurbarán on the Labors Hercules. Works showing achievements of th Hapsburgs, a family which ruled the Holy Roma Empire as well as Spain, were also commissione from other important artists. Velázquez's Surrer der of Breda is one of these. In addition, a group paintings by Italian artists depicting events in th history of Rome was included in the decoratio The program at Buen Retiro was completed by

ANTHONY VAN DYCK.
Portrait of Sir Endymion Porter, with the Artist.
c. **1632-41. Prado Museum, Madrid.**
The self-portrait takes on a new dimension here, with the placement of the artist beside the major subject. Porter, secretary to the Duke of Buckingham, was a connoisseur and collector of paintings. By including his own image next to that of an important person, Van Dyck announced his own position as a painter to be noble.

ries of coats of arms and portraits of the Spanish ings.

The more complex imagery in decorative chemes such as these was appreciated only by he culturally elite. Well-known stories or figures om history and mythology had a wider appeal. he identification of the king with Hercules, for istance, was readily understood by the general ublic.

The mix of ideas, styles, and themes in Baoque painting is difficult to sort out. No common ule can be applied to the various trends, espeially since the supporters of each trend had their

63

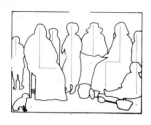

**LOUIS LE NAIN.
Drawing from *Peasant
Family in an Interior*.
c. 1642. The Louvre,
Paris.**

Some Realist artists treated
separate elements within a
painting individually. The
figures here are isolated
from one another, and
placed in a framework of
straight lines and right
angles. The resulting composition is somewhat static
and diffuse, but it conveys
a powerful impression of
observed reality. This
impression is usually created most effectively by
attention to details. The
viewer is encouraged to
dwell on details instead of
on the composition as
a whole.

own ideas about the best way to convey their me
sage. Reason and sentiment, intellectualism a
persuasion all had their champions. In the real
of form, the great argument was between t
advocates of drawing, or line, and those of pair
ing, or color. In general, Baroque painting copi
16th-century Venetian models, which eliminat
sharp contours and, instead, blurred the lin
between objects. The brushwork was free, in co
trast to the linear approach of the Renaissanc
Yet the value of drawing was not complete
ignored. Classicists such as Poussin concentrat
on the perfection of drawing technique. Son
Realist and Naturalist painters, too, used a sharp
line, because of their interest in the careful depi
tion of details.

Variety also exists in the disposition of elemen
within a painting. High Baroque compositio
were usually open and dynamic, with individu
objects or figures seemingly propelled by son
internal force to the edges of the frame. Hig
Baroque painting communicates a totality rath
than giving information about individual aspec
of a subject.

Some stylistic trends within Baroque paintin
did not exhibit the same focus on unity, howeve
The Naturalist/Realist movement emphasize
details. Straight lines and static geometric form
sometimes took precedence over curves, diag
nals, spirals, and other dynamic shapes, so th
compositional technique did not divert attentio

IEGO VELÁZQUEZ.
as Meninas. 1656.
rado Museum, Madrid.

his scene is structured
d united through the use
color and light. The gos-
mer effect of this light
prevents the whole from
breaking down into indi-
vidual parts. Instead, the
atmosphere unites the disparate elements of the
painting, while the ques-
tions raised by this painting
about the nature of vision
and pictorial reality give it
a cryptic quality.

GERRIT VAN HONTHORST. *The Concert.* **1620. Uffizi Gallery, Florence.**
Painters of the School of Utrecht, including Honthorst and the French painter de La Tour, were interested in lighting effects. Here two light sources are included in the scene, each illuminating a group of figures. The light becomes an active element in the composition, emphasizing textures and giving solid form to the figures.

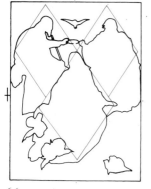

DIEGO VELÁZQUEZ. Drawing from *The Coronation of the Virgin.* **1641-42. Prado Museum, Madrid.**
Velázquez was a master of the geometrical arrangement of elements within his compositions. *Coronation of the Virgin*, inspired by a woodcut by Albrecht Dürer, is based on three large diamond-shaped forms. This work shows that High Baroque paintings can adhere to strict rules of composition.

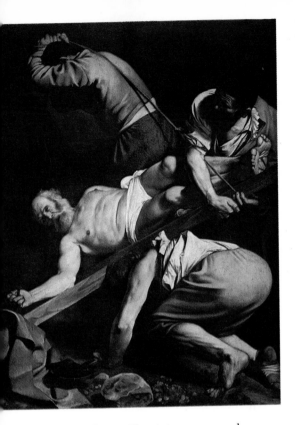

way from the subject. Classicists, too, used a system of groupings, which were dynamic in themselves, yet stood out as individual elements within the whole.

The rational arrangement of figures and objects which seems so clear in Classical works can be found in High Baroque painting as well; although its presence is not so easy to detect. Rubens's style, however, is as much based on geometric forms as that of Poussin. These structures are simply masked by the richness of the brushwork and the dynamism of the composition.

Some aspects of Baroque composition depend on the subject as much as on the stylistic preferences of the artist. The **horizon line**, for example, was adjusted to suit the meaning of a painting. A

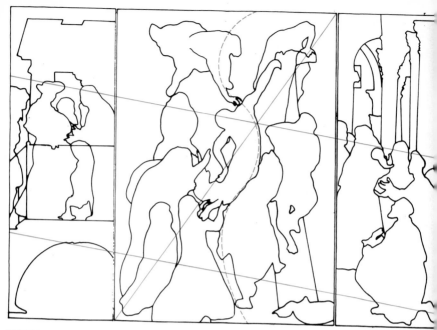

**PETER PAUL RUBENS.
Drawing from *The
Descent from the Cross*.
Antwerp Cathedral,
Antwerp.**

This High Baroque composition is made up of a system of diagonals and convex/concave curves, which give the triptych, or three-paneled painting, unity. The diagonals create a movement from the upper left to the lower right and serve to connect the three sections that make up the triptych.

low skyline was often used to emphasize figure especially saints in ecstasy or undergoing phys cal changes. Other subjects were represented wit a medium to low horizon.

An essential part of all Baroque painting is ligh Baroque artists largely abandoned the Renais sance practice of centralizing a single subject choosing instead to establish several focal point within a work. Chiaroscuro contributed to thi process by illuminating the most important par of a scene or by creating several areas of nearl equal interest. Caravaggio preferred to spotligh certain elements in his works with an artificiall strong light which enhanced the mood of the paintings. In Realist art, chiaroscuro strengthened rather than diminished the sense of reality.

General illumination could also be made to serve a compositional purpose. Lorrain, a painter of Classical landscapes, used light to create a

poetic atmosphere for his scenes of antiquity. The Dutch painter, Vermeer, used light as a subject in itself, foreshadowing the interests of the Impressionists of the late 19th century.

Colors varied according to geographical region and stylistic preference. Ochre tones, earthy red and yellow, predominated in Spanish paintings, while cooler colors can be found in Flemish works. The High Baroque generally made use of warm colors of high value, that is, suffused with light. These were intended to have an emotional effect upon the viewer. Poussin and the Classicists employed cooler colors in order to create a detached, rational effect.

CLAUDE LORRAIN.
Fording a River. **c. 1635.**
Prado Museum, Madrid.
The French painter Claude Lorrain used atmosphere and light to give unity to his compositions and to evoke the poetic world of antiquity. In his works, a luminous haze lies over the countryside, creating a sense of mystery. Human beings and animals seem almost submerged in the landscape.

FRANCISCO DE HERRERA. *Apotheosis of Saint Hermengild.* **1654. Prado Museum, Madrid.**

This work exhibits the boldness of the High Baroque style. The arched back of the central figure creates a dynamic rhythm of curves which carry him upward. The sensation of weightlessness is accentuated by the other figures moving through space with the saint. An unreal light shows the divine nature of the event and helps to glorify the subject. A group of bishops, arranged in a triangle, cowers in the darkness which symbolizes the obscurity of their doctrine.

It is this diversity of styles and approaches which makes the Baroque period so fascinating. Reason and sentiment vied for dominance in painting and sculpture. Imagination, symbolism, realism, and decoration could be used in combination or in conflict with each other. This variety mirrored the spirit of the age—contradictory, yet tied to tradition.

DRAWINGS AND PRINTS

Drawing and print making often represent different phases in the production of a work of art. The first may involve a preliminary stage, the second an interpretation of a completed work. However, many drawings stand on their own and never become the basis for paintings or sculptures. Prints, too, can be original works of art rather than copies of something else. Both can have great artistic value.

Drawings were used mainly for preliminary studies in the 17th century, although the drawings of famous artists were already valued and collected. Prints, on the other hand, served many different purposes. Easy reproduction made them an ideal vehicle for dispersing new styles and for recording the appearance of objects and animals. Thus they had an educational function for scientists as well as artists. Academies used prints to

PETER PAUL RUBENS.
The Birth of Apollo.
Prado Museum, Madrid.
The spontaneity of Baroque
drawings is sometimes at
odds with the pomposity of
finished paintings and
sculpture. Rubens, whose
works are often overly elaborate and complex, pro-
duces a simple and lively
composition here. The
flowing, curved lines give
the impression of great
naturalness and spontaneity.

teach architecture and anatomy and to make st∎
dents familiar with important works of art. ∎
individual sheets, or in collection, prints were als∎
available to the general public and were used ∎
decorate the homes of the wealthy and the mi∎
dle classes.

Rubens and Rembrandt are among the greates∎
print makers of the 17th century. Rembrandt ∎
considered the most creative. He experimented ∎
great deal in his prints, and often ignored the tra∎
ditional mass-production techniques preferred b∎
those who did the actual printing. These printer∎
naturally wanted to get as many prints as possi∎
ble from a plate and the bold, coarse lines use∎
by most artists suited their needs well. Rem∎
brandt, however, was interested in the fine∎
nuances of shading which could be obtained b∎
varying the depth and width of the lines.

DECORATIVE ARTS

Catalan Plate. 17th century. Museum of Catalan Art, Barcelona. Important developments occurred in ceramic making during this period, especially in Spain, Italy, France, and Germany. This plate shows the same interest in mythological themes found in other arts.

The decorative arts acquired great importance during the 17th century. Middle-class homes, as well as aristocratic houses and palaces, had to be filled with objects in keeping with the rank and social position of the occupants. The design of furniture, carpets, household equipment, jewelry, and clothing were subject to current styles and fashions.

Furniture design changed greatly during this period. The commode, or chest of drawers, inlaid

with **marquetry** and adorned with precious metals, made its appearance in France during the
reign of Louis XIV. Chairs became less intricate,
less elegant, and S-shaped outlines were adopted.

Tapestries, which adorned the walls of many
residences, were based on designs made by painters. Cartoons, or full-scale preparatory drawing

**ELOY CAMANYES and
AUGUSTIN ROCA.
Monstrance. 1638.
Cathedral Treasury,
Tortosa.**

This magnificent piece, a
vessel for communion
wafers, is an example of the
many gold and silver
objects made in the 17th
century and intended for
religious use. Based on
15th-century models and
containing details of decoration that are almost
Mannerist, it nevertheless
reflects contemporary
Baroque taste.

**SALVADOR RIERA.
Pendant. 1699. Museum
of the History of the City,
Barcelona.**
Baroque style is often beautifully expressed in jewelry.
Complex forms and the use
of many different materials
were the essence of well-
made 17th-century jewelry.

Apprentices' design books
have left many drawings,
which help art historians
assess the artistic merits of
individual pieces and the
fashions which influenced
them.

ere done by artists and given to weavers who
anslated the scenes into textile form. The
obelins in Paris and various Flemish factories
ere the chief producers of tapestries.

Ceramics and glassware were considered house-
old utensils, but there were great differences in
uality between objects intended for the use of
ie privileged classes and those for the use of the
wer classes. The workshops of Faience, Tal-
era, Delft, and Haarlem supplied much of the
emand. The best crystal, however, came from
ie Murano works in Venice and from Bohemia.
Works from precious metals have already been
entioned in the section on sculpture. Yet there
e many decorative objects and jewelry from the
aroque period which are as worthy of study as
arble or bronze sculpture. Numerous works in

**Drawings from
armchairs of the periods
of Henry IV, Louis XIII,
and Louis XIV.**
These chairs show the evolution of furniture design in
17th-century France, from
the intricate Renaissance
forms of the reign of Henry
IV, through the heavy
Louis XIII types, to the bul-
bous shapes and brackets
of the Louis XIV style. At
its height, French furniture
design represented an alli-
ance of all the arts.

gold, silver, and other precious materials we
made for the Catholic Church to be used in cer
monies or as decoration. Santiago de Composte
was a main center of production in Spain, but tl
finest items of gold, silver, and jewelry came fro
France. Coins, while obviously related to secul;
culture rather than religious practice, also fo
lowed Baroque fashion.

In conclusion, Baroque art should not l
viewed as a single, undifferentiated entity, but ;
a mix of diverse trends. These come together 1
produce a distinctive style which reflects the co
tradictions and the search for unity of the 17
century.

GLOSSARY

Academic Classicism: the style of art that
developed in France during the reign of
Louis XIV and was quite formalized and
technically correct

Annunciation: in Christian doctrine, the
angel's announcement to the Virgin Mary
that she would give birth to the Christ
child

bambocciate: small paintings produce
by mostly northern European artist
which portray the lower classes as pi
turesque, somewhat violent, and/or ridi
ulous

chiaroscuro: the strong contrast of ligl
and shade in a pictorial work of art

Classicism: the style embodied in the art of ancient Greece and Rome, which stressed technical mastery, order, and an idealized treatment of mythological themes

Council of Trent: a series of conferences between 1545 and 1563 in which the Roman Catholic Church reformed worship practices and attempted to counteract Protestant teachings and define Catholic beliefs

dilettanti: artists who used the plastic arts to explore their own intellectual interests; amateur artists

Eucharist: the Christian sacrament of communion

High Baroque: a style of art, marked by extravagant forms and elaborate ornamentation, that stresses the emotion and drama of the entire composition

Holy Inquisition: the Roman Catholic tribunal for the discovery and punishment of heresy

Holy Week: the week between Palm Sunday and Easter during which Christians commemorate the last days before the crucifixion of Christ

horizon line: the line of demarcation between the earth and the sky

idolatry: worshipping a physical object as a god

Mannerism: the style of art that is characterized by spacial incongruity and the artificial elongation of human figures

marquetry: decorative work in which elaborate designs are formed by pieces of wood, shell, or ivory inlaid in wood veneer

Naturalism: a style of art which stressed common, everyday subjects treated in an unidealized manner

patron: the supporter of an artist, who may be a wealthy member of the nobility or middle class, or may be an institution such as the Catholic Church

plastic arts: the visual arts, such as painting and sculpture, especially as distinguished from written arts, such as music and poetry

quadratura: the illusionistic enhancement of architecture, which, by three-dimensional painting, makes a space seem larger than it actually is

Realism: the style of art which, like Naturalism, was true to accurate representation of everyday life, but which stressed detail to a greater degree

Rococo: the style of art that is characterized by fancifully curved forms and ornate ornamentation

theatrum sacrum: a stage on which to display painting and sculpture, literally a sacred theatre

ART THROUGHOUT THE AGES

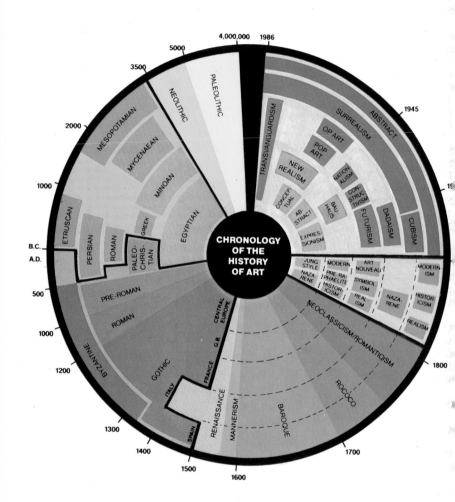

CHRONOLOGY OF THE HISTORY OF ART

This chart shows the evolution of Western and Near Eastern art through the ages. The terms are those that art historians traditionally use to label periods of time in various cultures where definite stylistic tendencies have occurred. The books in the Key to Art series examine the interplay of artists, ideas, methods and cultural influences that have affected the evolution of specific art styles.

INDEX OF ILLUSTRATIONS

CONTENTS

Acknowledgments
Aisa: pp. 33, 34, 52; Alte Pinakothek, Munich: p. 7; A.P.: pp. 35, 36, 43, 72; The British Museum, London: pp. 8, 71; F. Catalá-Roca: p. 39; Giraudon: pp. 18, 23, 44; Index: p. 74; Museum of Catalan Art, Barcelona: p. 75; The National Gallery, London: p. 58; The National Gallery of Scotland, Edinburgh: p. 51; Oronoz: pp. 28, 40; Prado Museum, Madrid: pp. 10, 57, 62, 63, 65, 69, 70; Réunion des Musées Nationaux: pp. 3, 21, 32, 46, 48, 50, 55, 59, 61; Rijksmuseum, Amsterdam: pp. 54, 60; Scala: pp. 5, 9, 12, 17, 19, 21, 24, 26-27, 30, 31, 37, 38, 41, 42, 45, 46; 56, 66, 67.